William Bolcom

Night Pieces

Five Preludes for Piano

ISBN 978-1-4950-8345-7

EDWARD B. MARKS MUSIC COMPANY / HAL•LEONARD®

EXCLUSIVELY DISTRIBUTED BY

7777 W. BLUEMOUND RD. P.O. BOX 13819 MILWAUKEE, WI 53213

www.ebmarks.com
www.halleonard.com

Night Pieces

The notes for my *Fantasy-Sonata* describe the overwhelming experience I had undergone at Pierre Boulez's Domaine Musical concerts, as well as those of the French Radio (ORTF) that also specialized in the very newest music (a year-old piece was already passé). Although there seemed little interest in the Boulez-Stockhausen-Berio musical world in the U.S. when I returned in 1961, I would as pianist set out to rectify this omission, then only successfully on the West Coast.

Night Pieces was written in Paris, shortly after I began my acquaintance with the current European international style, and premiered there. I never, however, wanted to eschew any musical reference from the past, including tonailty as so many composers did then—and the first sound in the pieces is a C-major triad, in 1960 a shocking chord. What I did absorb from the prevailing style was its liberation from regular meter, and the gestural language is largely derived from Boulez and related piano music. (The reference to Schoenberg in the last prelude is an hommage.)

David Chaitkin, the dedicatee, also lived at the Cité Universitaire when I was there. A fine composer, not well known enough; he passed away in 2011.

to David Chaitkin on his forthcoming marriage

Night Pieces
Five Preludes for Piano

William Bolcom
(1960)

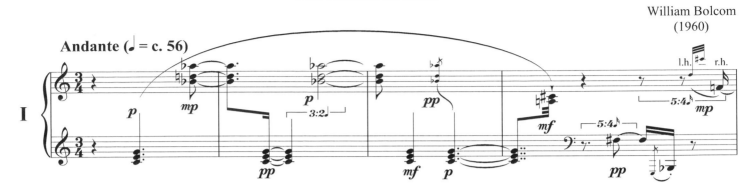

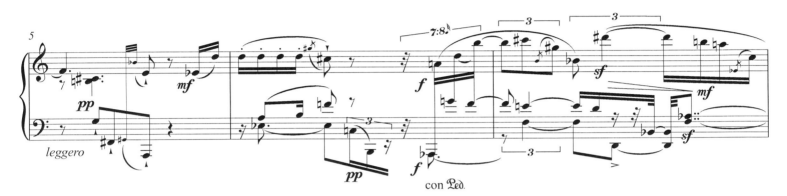

* $\boxed{\cdot}$ = short fermata

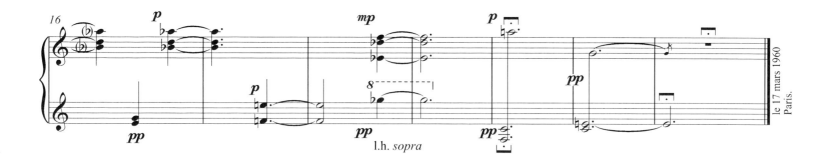

le 17 mars 1960
Paris.

II

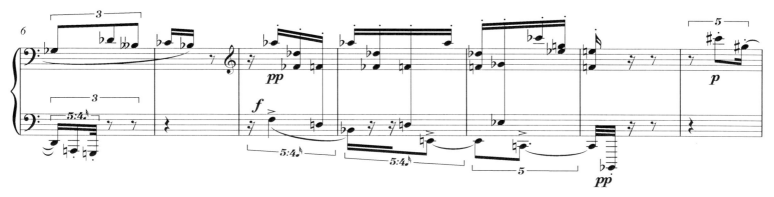

le 19 mars 1960
Paris.

* The + sign always goes toward "louder," i.e. "+pp" is louder than "pp."

6

Sostenuto (♩ = 48-52)

III(IIa)

una corda

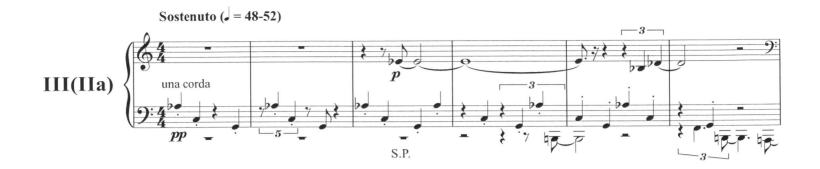

pp

S.P.

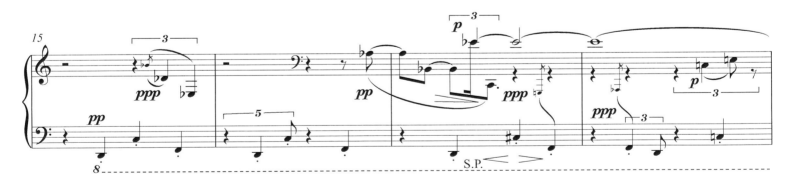

le 22 mars 1960

* Conversely, the - sign goes toward "softer."

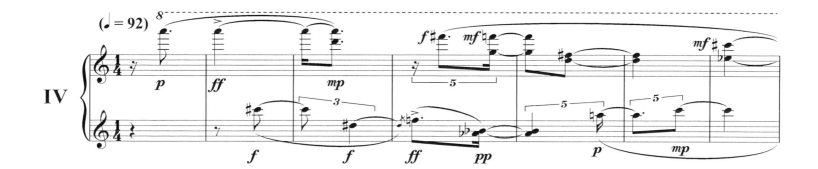

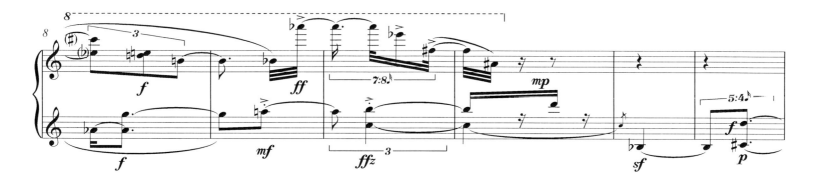

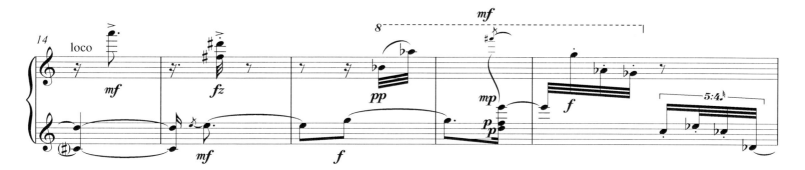

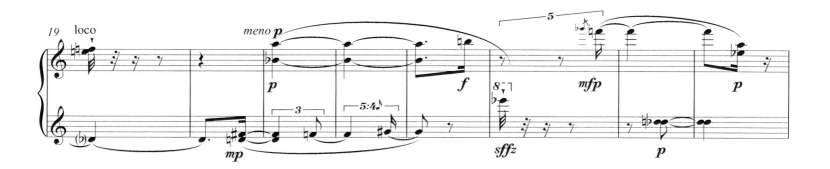

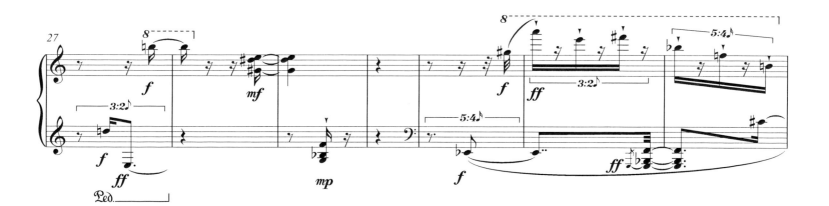

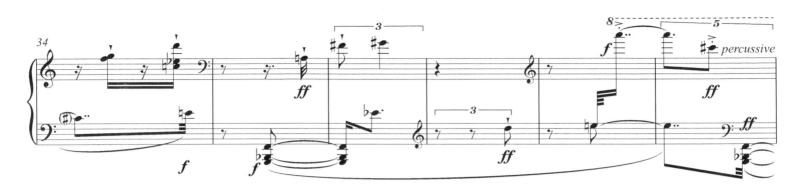

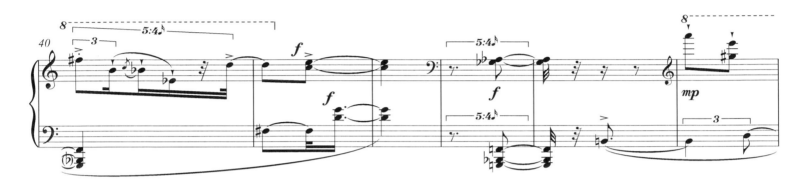

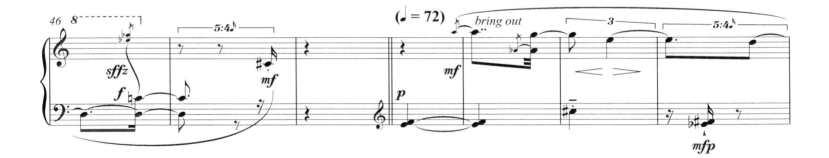

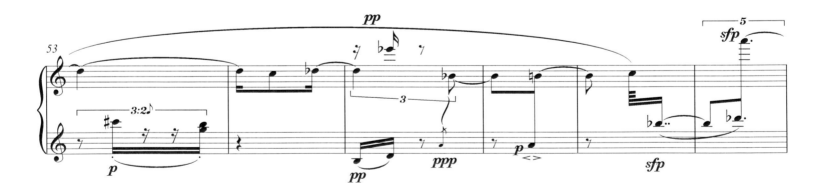

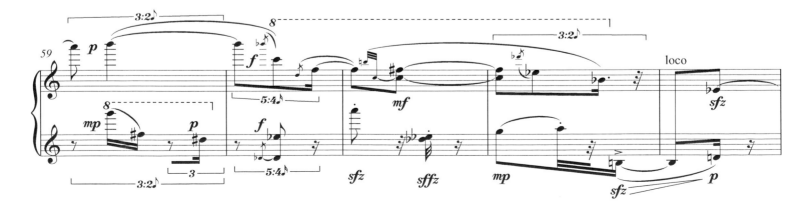

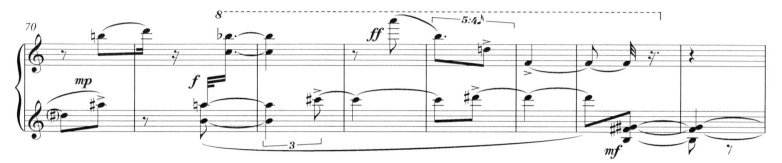

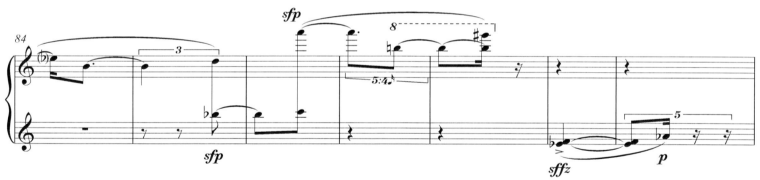

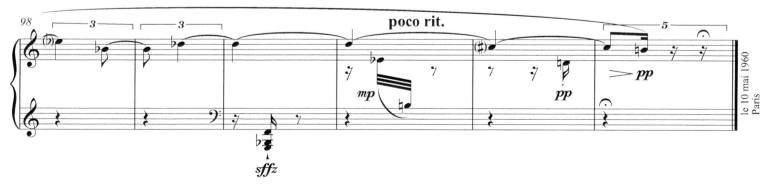

le 10 mai 1960
Paris

Largo (♩ = 40 - 60 circa)

V

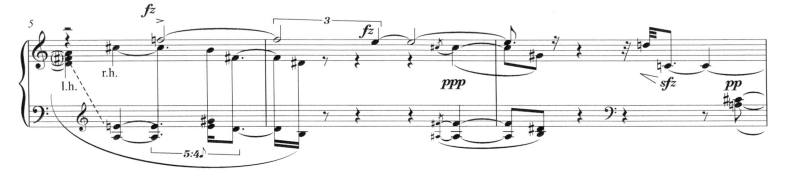

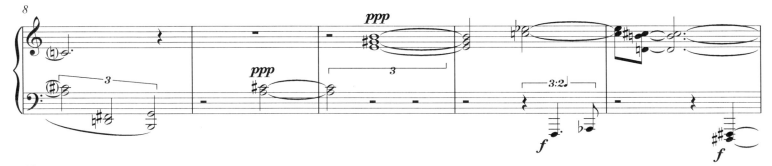

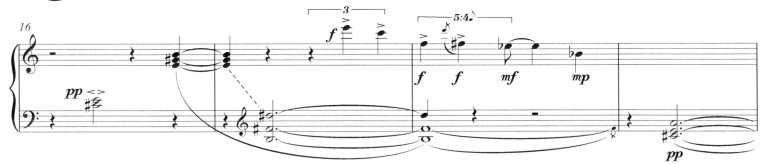

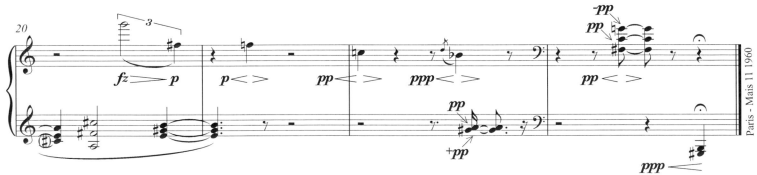

Paris - Mais 11 1960

March - May 1960